Exploring the Ancient World

ANCIENT ROME

Sean Sheehan and Pat Levy

Gareth Stevens
Publishing

Please visit our Web site, www.garethstevens.com. For a free color catalog of all our high-quality books, call toll free 1-800-542-2595 or fax 1-877-542-2596.

Library of Congress Cataloging-in-Publication Data

Sheehan, Sean, 1951-
Ancient Rome / Sean Sheehan and Pat Levy.
    p. cm. — (Exploring the ancient world)
Includes bibliographical references and index.
ISBN 978-1-4339-4160-3 (library binding)
1. Rome—Civilization—Juvenile literature. I. Levy, Patricia, 1951- II. Title.
DG77.S46 2011
937—dc22

                        2010014427

This edition first published in 2011 by
Gareth Stevens Publishing
111 East 14th Street, Suite 349
New York, NY 10003

Editorial Director: Kerri O'Donnell
Art Director: Haley Harasymiw

Photo Credits:
Bridgeman Art Library *cover*, 1 (Archaeological Museum, Naples), Ronald Sheridan Ancient Art and Architecture Collection Ltd. 8
9, 16, 17, 20–21, 25, 26, 32, 33, 34, 39, 42–43, 46, 48, 59 (middle); C. M. Dixon 5, 10, 12 (top), 12 (bottom), 15, 18, 22, 24–25 (middle), 2
28–29, 30, 37 (top), 41, 44, 47, 51, 52, 54, 59 (top); E. T. Archive, 6, 7 (Archaeological Museum, Naples), 35 (Prestino Museum, Rome
36, 49 (National Glyptothek, Munich), 53 (bottom right), 56 (San Vitale, Ravenna Italy); Werner Forman Archive 31, 45, 50 (J. Paul (
Museum, Malibu), 55, 60.

Printed in China
CPSIA compliance information: Batch #WAS10GS: For further information contact Gareth Stevens, New York, New York at 1-800-542-2595.

Contents

Early Rome

In the space of 1,000 years, ancient Rome created the greatest empire that the world has ever seen. It was not only the size of the empire that was so impressive, but also its ability to take on all the best aspects of the cultures that it conquered. Even 1,500 years after the fall of Rome, its legacy survives in the languages, architecture, laws, and thinking of today. Ancient Roman civilization is still regarded as one of the great ages of humankind.

At the time that ancient Rome was beginning to expand its territories, many Mediterranean countries were made up of farming communities. In neighboring Greece there was an advanced culture, but the Greeks wasted a lot of time on civil wars. They had never colonized the other lands around them, apart from some colonies in southern Italy. Other peoples, like the Etruscans, were exploring new lands, settling in the plains of Italy, north and south of the Tiber River. It was Rome, however, that became the most important city in Italy.

▼ **This map shows Italy in the early days of Rome, around 750 BCE. It was inhabited by immigrants from Greece, North Africa, and Europe. Rome was just one of many small settlements, yet it was Rome that eventually dominated the area.**

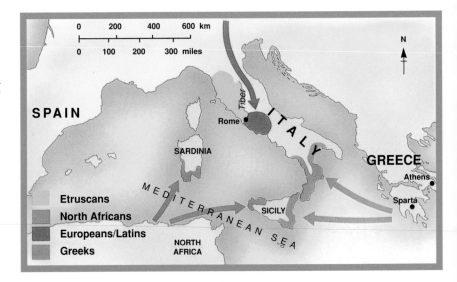

Italy is in the center of the Mediterranean; it has a long coastline, making links with Greece, Africa, and Spain possible by sea. This put Italy in a central position to develop trade in the region. Rome itself was in the fertile valley of the Tiber River, in a warm climate. Inland it was easy to defend, with the natural defenses of the seven hills, but at the same time, the river gave it access to the sea for war and trading. Much of the rest of Italy is mountainous. All around Rome were other peoples who wanted more land, so at first Rome went to war only to defend its land. Rome first drove other competing cultures out of Italy, made peace with the conquered tribes, and then set out to destroy their competitors farther afield.

▼ *The center of the Roman Empire—the Forum in Rome. The three pillars are the remains of the temple to Castor and Pollux, and behind it is the Curia, where the Roman senate met.*

Legends and Origins

The story of ancient Rome began around 800 BCE, in a small settlement on one of the seven hills of Rome; but historians do not know how, or exactly when, this first settlement developed.

In one legend, there was a king named Numitor. His sons were killed by his jealous brother, Amulius, who then made Numitor's daughter, Rhea Silvia, become a priestess. After Mars, the god of war, fell in love with her, Rhea had twin sons, Romulus and Remus. When Amulius found out, he threw Rhea and her babies into the Tiber. A female wolf found the twins and brought them up. Years later, a shepherd discovered them and brought them to Numitor, where the whole story was explained.

Amulius was killed in battle, so the twins decided to build a new city to celebrate his death. An oracle told them to build the city on the Palatine Hill; it also said that Romulus was to be the king of the city. Romulus took a plow and plowed a line to show the city's boundaries. Remus, now jealous of his brother, jumped over the furrow to disobey his brother and Romulus killed him. Romulus then became the first king of Rome.

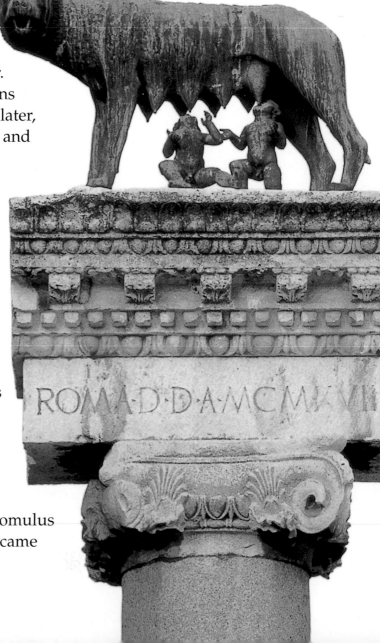

▼ *In* The Early History of Rome *Livy writes: "A she-wolf, coming down from the neighboring hills... heard the children... she treated them with such gentleness that Faustulus, the king's herdsman, found her licking them with her tongue."*

ROMA·D·D·A·MC·M·XVII

▶ *In this fresco from Pompeii, Aeneas, the ancestor of Romulus and Remus, is having his wounds dressed after the battle at Troy.*

Historians know that the first people to live on the Palatine Hill were Latin peoples from northern Italy. They lived in small oblong huts made of wooden poles, woven around with twigs and branches and filled in with clay. They herded sheep and cattle and kept goats and pigs. Their burial ground was at the foot of the Palatine Hill. Each of the seven hills of Rome was probably a separate village. In the very early history of Rome, these Latin people were invaded by Etruscans from the north, who became their kings. They united the seven hills into one city and brought their skills as builders and artists to this new city.

Another legend says that a famous warrior from Troy, Aeneas, was the ancestor of Romulus and Remus. Aeneas fled Troy after its defeat at the hands of the Greeks, and he sailed around the world, having many adventures. Eventually he arrived in Italy and settled there. His story is told in the Aeneid, a famous Roman poem written by Virgil. Here is a part of the story where he first sees Rome: "Now Aeneas, looking out from the glassy ocean, sees a vast stretch of forest. The Tiber River's pleasant stream flows through it before bursting into the sea in swirling eddies. Above and all around, different birds sweeten the air with song. Having ordered his companions to change course and steer for land, Aeneas is elated as he makes the river's shade."

s

...o be the first king of Rome in 753 ...d by six more kings until 510 BCE, ... a Republic. These kings began to ...ortant city. First, they expanded ... a neighboring city, Alba Longa. Then the sixth king, Servius Tullius, made Rome into a religious center by building a shrine to Diana, the hunter goddess. His son, Tarquinius Superbus, built a huge temple to Jupiter, the king of the gods. Rome soon became an important religious site.

The kings of Rome were very powerful people. They were in charge of war, public buildings, and religion. They also acted as city judges. Everywhere they went, their assistants carried a bundle of rods with an ax in the middle, known as a *fasces*, to show that the king had the power to have anyone executed or beaten. Servius Tullius was the first Roman king to have coins made. Before this, cows had been used as money; one cow was equal to ten sheep. Later, for convenience, people began to use bronze bars as money. Finally, a standard bronze coin stamped with a cow's head became the currency.

1084.—Roman Lictor.

▲ *The kings of Rome were accompanied by a servant, called a* lictor, *who carried the symbols of power, the bundle of rods and an ax, the* fasces.

It is thought that the Etruscans first came to Italy from the east, from what is now Turkey, and that they were influenced by the Greeks, with whom they traded. At the height of their civilization, they ruled nearly all of Italy, and they made important contributions to the history of Rome. Examples of their art and technology show them to be a talented and creative people; but their separate identity was gradually lost as Rome grew more important. Historians are still unable to translate the examples of their writing that survive.

The kings also commissioned Rome's famous system of sewers. At first people had used the streams that ran between the seven hills of the city to carry waste water away, but then they began to build huge underground sewers.

However, the kings became too ruthless. The last king of all, Tarquinius Superbus, forced the citizens to give up their own work to work for him. A later Roman historian tells the story:

"The poor were set to work in return for a miserable ration of grain: quarrying stone, cutting timber, leading the wagons, or even themselves carrying the materials on their backs. Various craftsmen, coppersmiths, carpenters, and stonemasons were all forcibly removed from their private business to labor for the public good."

A group of noblemen led a rebellion, and Tarquinius, the last Etruscan king of Rome, had to escape from the city with his supporters. The exact year of this event is not known, but it is believed to have been around 510 BCE. The people, having got rid of their kings, set up a republic, meaning "rule by the people," which was headed by two consuls elected each year.

► *This bronze jug from the fourth century* BCE *shows the skilled craftsmanship of the Etruscan people.*

9

Republic to Empire

The Republic

After 510 BCE, the Romans set up a new government based on wealth. At the head of the government were two consuls; they were elected by wealthy men from the senate for periods of one year. The senate was elected from the richest and most important men, and its job was to advise the two consuls. The poor were called the plebs, or plebeians, and at first they had no say in government. But in 490 BCE, they held a protest on one of the small hills outside Rome. The leaders of Rome needed the plebeians to fight in their armies, so they had to agree to give them some power. They allowed them to elect two representatives, called tribunes, to speak for them. These tribunes became very powerful and could keep laws from being passed if they disagreed with them. Later, the number of tribunes was increased to ten, and the plebeians were allowed to run for other government positions. After 367 BCE, one of the consuls was elected from among the plebeians, rather than from the wealthier classes.

Meanwhile, other cities in Italy were forming alliances against Rome.

▶ *A bronze statue of a Gaulish warrior from the Imperial Period of Rome's history. His ancestors overran Rome in 386 BCE.*

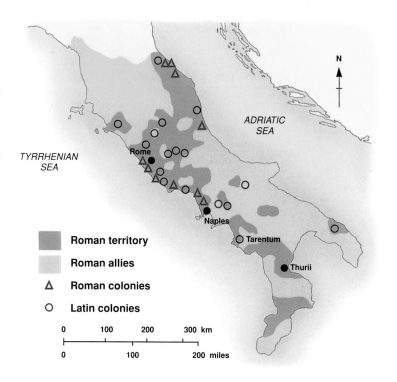

In 496 BCE, Rome was attacked and forced to join an alliance of Latin cities. Gradually Rome took over that alliance. Then in 386 BCE, the Gauls, from northern Europe, attacked and destroyed Rome; after their victory, they stayed in Rome for a few months. In the end, the Romans had to pay the Gauls in gold to persuade them to leave the city. The Romans rebuilt their city and constructed a strong wall around the seven hills. It was at this time that they began wars against other cities in Italy. The first of these was against the people who had once ruled them, the Etruscans.

Rome gradually captured more territory and built up an empire; by 264 BCE, Rome dominated Italy. In some cities they allowed the local population to become Roman citizens. Often local people had to give up some of their land for Roman settlers to live on. Many cities were allowed to trade with Rome, but they were not allowed to trade with anyone else. Sometimes citizens from captured territories could even marry Romans. All of these territories had to supply soldiers for Rome's army.

▲ **This map shows how far Roman territory had expanded by about 264 BCE.**

In 451 BCE, a committee drew up a set of laws for the city. The laws were written on 12 bronze plaques and displayed in the city center. They remained the law throughout the history of the Roman Empire. They covered many aspects of life, and everyone had to obey them. Among other things, they laid down the punishments for murder, prohibited cremations within the city, dictated the width of roads, and allowed fathers to kill their deformed children.

War Against Carthage

In the north of Africa, another great city was flourishing. Carthage had colonies all over the Mediterranean and, using its fleet of warships, it traded deep into Africa and even as far as Britain. Whenever the Carthaginians came across Roman boats, they rammed them and sank them.

In 264 BCE war broke out between Carthage and Rome on the island of Sicily. Although it began over a fairly petty incident, it was the first in a series of wars that propelled Rome into a position of great power. The Carthaginians occupied a small trading post on Sicily. The Romans attacked and drove them out, which enraged the rulers of Carthage. A war at sea began between Rome and Carthage, and the Romans had to build ships quickly to match the might of the Carthaginian fleet. The Roman boats had sharp spikes in front that were let down before ramming the Carthaginian boat, locking the boats together and allowing troops to rush aboard the enemy ship. In 241 BCE, the Romans won the first war; they then invaded Carthaginian colonies on Corsica and Sardinia.

▲ *This terra-cotta plaque shows a war elephant like those used by Hannibal on his trip across the Alps. One of their most useful functions was to frighten the local tribes, who were afraid to attack such huge creatures.*

▼ *This mosaic shows a Roman warship. These ships had an underwater ram, used for breaking holes in the enemy's ships. The eye of Osiris on the front of the boat was to ward off disease.*

▶ *In 204 BCE, the Roman general, Scipio, invaded Africa and met the Carthaginian leader, Hannibal, in battle. Scipio defeated Hannibal who was recalled to defend his homeland. Scipio was given the name "Africanus," as a reward for his great victory.*

In 218 BCE, a second war broke out, this time involving the famous Carthaginian general, Hannibal, who led his troops from Spain over the Alps to Italy. Hannibal's troops traveled to an area south of Rome where they were based for 14 years and where they engaged in many wars with Roman troops. In 202 BCE, Hannibal took his troops back to Africa to defend Carthage against Roman troops. He was defeated at the battle of Zama, and Carthage surrendered. Rome gave the Carthaginians a restricted area of territory, made them surrender most of their ships and armor, and imposed a heavy fine on them. Carthage was now much less powerful as an empire, yet the Romans were still not satisfied. They began a third war with Carthage in 149 BCE, and this time they did not stop until the city was destroyed. Some stories say that the Romans even sowed the fields of Carthage with salt, making them useless for agriculture. The 50,000 survivors in the city were sold as slaves.

Hannibal became a general at the age of 26. He knew that Rome had hundreds of ships and could easily beat him at sea, so he decided to force the Romans to fight on land. He marched his troops to the north of Spain, into France, and through the majestic Italian Alps into Italy. He had approximately 100,000 troops and 36 elephants. By midsummer he was in France; but he had lost 40,000 men, fighting against the tribes of Spain and France. Once he even had to blast his way through a rock wall by heating the rocks and then throwing cold wine on them in order to crack them. By the time Hannibal reached northern Italy, he had only 26,000 men left. Despite this, he still managed to defeat Roman armies twice. After Hannibal was called back to Carthage and defeated, he went into exile and spent the rest of his life as a hunted man.

GAUL

N

SPAIN

CORSICA

ITALY

Rome

Cannae

SARDINIA

SICILY

NORTH AFRICA

Carthage

Carthaginian Empire
Hannibal's march
Hannibal's return
Scipio's invasion

| 0 | 200 | 400 | 600 | 800 | km |
| 0 | 100 | 200 | 300 | 400 | 500 | miles |

The Civil Wars

In the 100 years following Hannibal's defeat, the Romans expanded their empire until it covered much of the land bordering the Mediterranean. The empire was ruled over by governors who grew very rich.

Back in Rome, wealthy soldiers began to spend lots of money bribing people to vote them into power. On the other hand, peasants who had fought in the wars against Carthage returned to find that their farms were ruined. The wealthy people bought up the farms and sent their slaves to work on them, while the homeless peasants drifted into Rome to find work. They became very discontented, and in 133 BCE, a tribune named Tiberius Gracchus suggested that the big farms be broken up and given back to the poor. The landowners and senators did not like this and started riots. Other plans to give out land to the poor were also stopped.

The poor people finally began to vote for consuls who would help them and oppose the powerful men of the senate. Civil war broke out in Rome in 88 BCE, and the senators took away the power of the tribunes.

Pompey first became consul in 70 BCE. In between his years as consul, he was a very successful general and won a lot of land for Rome; he also mounted a successful campaign against the pirates who were robbing Roman ships in the Mediterranean. He married Julius Caesar's daughter, Julia, but she died in childbirth five years later. One Roman writer, Lucan, suggested that if she had lived, Caesar and Pompey might have stayed friends rather than become enemies:
"Julia alone, if granted by the fates a longer life, could have restrained her resentful husband and her father, too; could have pushed aside their swords and joined the hands that held the weapons...Her death shattered family ties and released the enmity between the two."

In 62 BCE, a general named Pompey was made consul and restored the power of the tribunes. Another general at this time was Julius Caesar. In 51 BCE, after a series of successful campaigns there, Caesar was given command of Gaul. For a while these two men, with the help of a third, named Crassus, ruled Rome between them as consuls. They were known as the Triumvirate. Eventually, Crassus was murdered and Caesar decided to take power for himself. Caesar, still in charge of the territory of Gaul, was a very successful general and a great leader. He was popular with the poor, who supported him in politics. Pompey had the support of the senators.

In 49 BCE Caesar marched with his troops into Rome. Pompey and the senators withdrew to Greece, where they intended to plan a campaign against Caesar. But Caesar caught them, defeated Pompey, and chased him to Egypt. Before Caesar could take Pompey prisoner, his one-time friend was murdered by the Egyptians. Caesar stayed in Egypt, settling his affairs, until 45 BCE when he returned to Rome to take power.

▼ *Julius Caesar became sole ruler of Rome, and people began to fear his power. He was stabbed to death in 44 BCE by conspirators.*

The Roman Empire

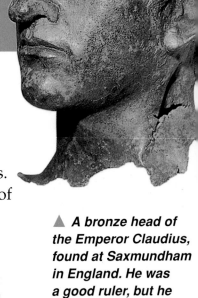

The Emperors

Julius Caesar was a particularly popular leader with the poorer people of Rome. He ordered marshland to be drained for the poor people to farm and arranged for others to get land in Rome's colonies. He also invented the Julian calendar, the predecessor of our modern calendar. But Caesar had many enemies among the rich and powerful, and only five months after he came to Rome he was murdered.

Caesar's nephew, Octavian, had to fight and defeat Mark Antony, who had been Julius Caesar's co-consul, before he could take on leadership of Rome. From then on, Octavian called himself Augustus Caesar. He was emperor until he died in 14 CE. It was under him that Rome became an empire; he still called the empire a republic, but he kept all the real powers of state for himself. He was a good ruler who improved the city, reorganized the army, and chose good governors for the Roman colonies. He had hundreds of miles of roads built to improve both trade and communications.

▲ A bronze head of the Emperor Claudius, found at Saxmundham in England. He was a good ruler, but he often drifted off into daydreams instead of performing his official duties.

Probably the worst emperor was Nero. At first he was so inexperienced that he wanted to abolish all taxes, so that people would like him. Later he made several attempts to have his mother killed; he did have two of his wives killed. He created two new public festivals at which everyone had to listen to him play and sing. Eventually the senate declared him a public enemy and Nero killed himself.

For 200 years after Augustus became emperor, the empire was at peace and people settled down to build new cities. When Augustus died, he was made a god.

Since the emperor was not a king and the title was not hereditary, anyone who had support from important people could come to power. The men who became emperors after Augustus were both good and bad. Caligula was so power-crazed that he made his horse a consul and built a marble stable for it. Claudius (who was found hiding behind a curtain in the imperial palace after the murder of Caligula) was proclaimed emperor. He developed into a serious and steady ruler. He expanded the civil service and increased the powers of imperial governors abroad. In 43 CE, he conquered Britain and even allowed important non-Romans across the empire to become Roman citizens. He died in suspicious circumstances in 54 CE, after eating poisonous mushrooms.

After this there were many emperors. In one year, 69 CE, there were four different emperors, three of whom were either assassinated or committed suicide. In 117 CE Hadrian became emperor. He was Spanish and was a brilliant general. He worked hard to improve the empire and not just expand it.

There were 66 emperors of Rome in all; the lengths of their reigns vary from 41 years to six months.

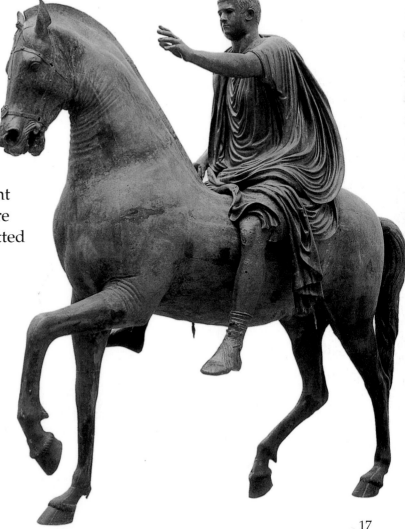

▼ **This statue shows Caligula and his horse. In three years Caligula wasted all the savings of his predecessor, Tiberius. For the first time in Roman history, taxes were imposed on the sale of food, a very unpopular measure.**

Expanding the Empire

After the time of the emperor Augustus, the Roman Empire expanded rapidly. Those who wanted jobs in the government in Rome had to prove their strength. They had to do so by conquering new territories or by stopping a rebellion in one of the colonies. Many of the Roman emperors added to the size of the empire during their reigns by conquering new land.

Julius Caesar had invaded Britain twice, in 55 BCE and 54 BCE, and while he was governor of Gaul from 58 BCE to 49 BCE he expanded Rome's territory to cover all of modern France.

In 31 BCE, Augustus, Caesar's adopted son, seized Egypt; the country had previously been an ally, but not part of the empire. He also expanded the empire in Europe, along the Rhine River and the Danube River, and put down rebellions in parts of Spain and the Alps. Claudius, who ruled from 41 CE to 54 CE, personally led a successful invasion of Britain. He also annexed Mauretania, in north Africa, and Thrace, along the shore of the Black Sea.

In 70 CE, under the emperor Vespasian, Jerusalem was attacked and made part of the empire. The empire grew to its biggest ever, between 98 CE and 117 CE, under the rule of Trajan. He sent his troops into large areas of the Middle East and modern Romania.

So, by 117 CE, the Roman Empire covered the whole coastline of north Africa, from Egypt to modern Morocco; all of Europe as far north as the Danube River, England, and Wales; modern Israel, and the Middle East as far east as the Tigris and Euphrates rivers.

▼ *At Hadrian's Wall, the outsides of the wall were stone banks. They were ten feet apart and filled with rubble and mortar. The wall was topped with battlements and a walkway for sentries.*

The borders of the Roman Empire stopped at natural barriers, such as the rivers of Europe, and the deserts of the Middle East. Where there was no natural boundary, in Britain and Germany, border walls were built to mark off conquered territories. The best example of a Roman border wall is Hadrian's Wall in England, which was the project of the Emperor Hadrian. It became obvious that Scotland would be too expensive to conquer, so Hadrian ordered that a 20-ft. (6-m)-high stone and turf wall be built across England, from the east coast to the west, about 73 mi. (117 km) in length. Sixteen large forts were built into the wall at regular intervals. Inside each fort lived between 500 and 1,000 soldiers. There were also 80 fortlets, called milecastles, which held between eight and 32 men, and there were lots of watchtowers, which could hold a few sentries. The towers, forts, and milecastles may have signaled to each other.

At Vindolanda, a Roman fort near Hadrian's Wall, a message, thought to be military intelligence, was found: "The Britons are unprotected by armor. There are very many cavalry. The cavalry do not use swords nor do the wretched Britons take up fixed positions in order to throw javelins."

Politics and Society

Government and Law

In the Roman Republic, the government was headed by two consuls who made the laws. They had absolute power, but either could challenge the acts of the other, and they had to agree before a change in the law was accepted. They were advised by the senate, which was originally made up only of rich men; these were the *patres*, or "fathers" of the community. Representatives of the common people, called tribunes, could block any measure proposed by a member of the senate. There were also two elected assemblies made up of the ordinary citizens of Rome; in theory these Roman citizens had an equal say in what went on in Rome, but in reality the assembly was controlled by the senate.

When the Emperor Augustus came to power in 27 BCE, he changed this system. There were still two consuls and a senate, but they could not pass laws—only the emperor could do that. The emperor had taken on the power of a consul, a tribune, and chief priest. He did not call himself emperor, but chose the title "first citizen."

▼ *The remains of the Basilica Aemilia in Rome. It was built in 179 CE by Aemilius Lepidus the censor. Basilicas were the public halls that lined Rome's forums or public squares. They were used for meetings or for shops and markets.*

This title gave him the right to speak first at senate meetings. Once he had said what he thought, no one dared to disagree, because Augustus had absolute power. He also chose all the senators and consuls. The assembly still met, but its job was to choose judges and agree to Augustus's laws; it was no longer a very powerful body. Every emperor after Augustus kept up this system of government.

The Twelve Tablets, which had been written in 451 BCE, were still in use in imperial times, but many more laws had been added to them. In the second century CE, the Emperor Hadrian decided that laws should be exactly the same all over the Roman Empire; so he ordered a lawyer to collect and write down all the laws. If a Roman citizen in Britain, Africa, or any other colony thought he had been mistreated in a courtroom in his own country, he could go to Rome to appeal against the ruling. Juries decided if someone was innocent or guilty. Sometimes a jury could have as many as 75 people.

In Rome, different people were punished in different ways for the same crime. A poor man would get a harsher punishment than a rich one. The courts distinguished between honestiores, wealthy or upper-class men, and humiliores, or poor men. A slave would nearly always get the worst punishment. No one went to prison in Roman society. For small crimes they paid fines, but for serious crimes they were banished or had their property taken away from them. If someone was sentenced to death that person was executed by crucifixion. Poor people were sent to the public games and died fighting a wild animal or another slave. The death sentence could be imposed for stealing crops or speaking unfairly about somebody, as well as for murder.

This mosaic from Ostia, the port of Rome, shows a man loading a merchant ship with amphorae. These pottery jugs would carry wine or oil. One of these ships could carry 6,000 or more amphorae. The ships varied in size from 60 ft. (18 m) to 100 ft. (30 m) long.

Trade

Trade was very important to the Roman Empire. The city of Rome produced very little of the basic things it needed, such as food, so these had to be imported from the colonies. Corn was the most important and biggest import; it was brought in from all over the empire: from North Africa, Spain, France, Great Britain, and the Middle East. Slaves were another very important product and were also imported from all over the empire. From Egypt came papyrus writing paper and from Dacia (modern Romania), Spain, and Great Britain came gold and silver. Glass came from Egypt, and linen cloth came from Arabia. Wine came from Gaul (modern France) and Spain. From Great Britain came delicacies like shellfish. Wild animals for the public shows and games came from Africa.

Rome also traded with countries that were not part of the empire, such as Poland, which traded amber, or modern Georgia, which traded cattle. Silk came from China, and spices, jewels, and perfumes came from India. From across the deserts, goods arrived at the Roman colonies on camel trains. The enormous network of roads carried wagons loaded with goods as far as the coasts; then trading ships, called *corbitae*, brought the goods across the sea. *Corbitae* were big, slow-moving ships and often had a huge, carved goose's head on the prow. The goose was the symbol of the goddess Isis, who was believed to protect sailors. Each ship had one big square mainsail and a smaller one at the front that was used to steer.

Pirates were a serious problem to Roman traders. In 67 BCE, ships in the Mediterranean were facing constant attacks. Pirates would board merchant ships and take their goods. Sailors who were citizens of the Roman Empire would be dressed up in Roman clothes and made to walk the plank; important rich men would be held for ransom. When the consul Pompey was a general, he was sent to rid the sea of the pirates. He was given 250 ships, 100,000 soldiers, and 4,000 cavalry. Within three months, he had taken thousands of prisoners and put all the pirates out of business.

Ships sailed between March and November, when there was less risk of storms at sea. At the mouths of major harbors, the Romans built lighthouses with fires burning at the top. When the ships arrived at the big Roman port of Ostia, the goods were unloaded onto flat-bottomed barges and carried up the Tiber River, to Rome.

▼ *This map shows the main trade routes used when the Roman Empire was at its height. Goods were carried from all corners of the empire and beyond, to Rome.*

Cattle	Gold	Fruit	Slaves
Wheat	Silver	Linen	Paper
Horses	Glass	Spices	Wool
Pottery	Wine	Silk	
Animals	Metal		
Seafood			

BRITAIN

GERMANIA

GAUL

SPAIN

ITALY

MACEDONIA

DACIA

BLACK SEA

GEORGIA

ASIA MINOR

FROM CHINA

FROM INDIA

MEDITERRANEAN SEA

MIDDLE EAST

NORTH AFRICA

EGYPT

Roman Empire

The Army

Rome had a very efficient army. In the early days of the Republic all men were called up in the event of an emergency. They left their work to go to battle and then went home—if they survived. Later, when the empire was big, the army had professional soldiers.

The professional Roman soldier went through a lengthy training session before he was ready to fight. He was trained in marching, riding, building a camp, stone slinging, and swimming. Weapons training was very important. Recruits practiced with heavy wooden swords and cane shields. They were also trained to throw wooden spears.

After training, the soldier joined a legion. Legionnaires were divided into four kinds of fighters. In battle the lowest rank, the *velites*, fought single-handedly. They had no body armor and carried light spears and shields. At the front of the battle line were the *hastati*. They wore light armor and carried a sword and two javelins. Behind them were the *principes*, who had swords, spears, and cylinder-shaped shields. At the back of the battle line were sword fighters called *triarii*. These were the most experienced soldiers and had spears and full body armor. They rarely fought because the ranks in front of them did most of the work.

▼ *This relief carving shows Roman soldiers in the battle against the Barbarians. They were cavalrymen, so they came from the wealthier Roman classes or were allies of the Romans.*

▶ *The Praetorian Guard was a 900-strong army. The Guard was created by the Emperor Augustus. They became very powerful, often choosing the next emperor in times of crisis. Behind them is their legionary standard— an eagle holding a thunderbolt in its claws.*

At Vindolanda (now called Chesterholm), a fort near Hadrian's Wall in England, a tiny scrap of a letter from home has been found. It says: "I have sent you...pairs of woolen socks, two pairs of sandals, and two pairs of underpants." On the cold border those things must have been very welcome.

At the flanks of the battle line were the cavalry. The Romans used cavalrymen, supplied by the local allies, wherever they were fighting. They wore full body armor and a helmet. In Hadrian's time the horses also wore armor. A Roman legionnaire joined up for 20 years. He was well paid and got bonuses if the army won a big victory. But his life was hard. He had to buy his own weapons, food, and clothes.

He had to march up to 20 mi. (30 km) a day. He carried a pack weighing about 65 lb (30 kg), including two huge stakes, which were used to build a defensive wall when the army made camp. At the end of the day's march, he had to help build the camp for the night. He carried three days' supply of rations, made up of whole-wheat biscuits, bacon, cheese, and wine. When soldiers were stationed at the frontiers, life got a little easier, with better food and even a chance to start a family with a local girl.

Ruling the Empire

As the Romans conquered more countries, they needed to make the people of those countries happy to be under Roman rule. Most of the countries they invaded consisted of small villages with basic technology. At first, the Romans built forts to control the local people, who might be restless after having been invaded. A fort contained barracks for the troops, houses for officers, workshops, granaries, and a hospital.

When a legionnaire retired after his 20 years of service, he was often given land near the fort where he could build his house. In this way towns developed around the forts. Roman engineers and architects built beautiful buildings, put in plumbing, and built aqueducts, temples, and wide roads. After the local people got used to the Romans, they often preferred the protection and amenities of town life to living in small isolated communities. In exchange for all these benefits, the people of the provinces paid taxes to support the army and to pay tribute to Rome.

▲ *In this Roman classroom the bearded figure in the middle is the teacher; on either side of him are his pupils. To the right is a slave, holding his young master's schoolbag. These boys learned to read and write in Latin.*

All over the empire, citizens paid taxes to Rome in exchange for protection and law and order. People paid taxes on the value of their homes and farms each year. Traveling tax inspectors visited every farm and house throughout the empire to decide how much they had to pay. Where soldiers were stationed in a town or village, the local people paid another type of tax in actual food for the soldiers. Also, as in many modern countries, the Romans paid taxes on the goods they bought and sold and on any wealth they inherited. At the height of the empire, this system ran well and was quite fair, but by the fourth century CE, the cost of running the empire and paying for the endless wars had become very high. This led to tax increases and the burden that they created added to civil unrest throughout the empire.

At first, the provinces traded their raw materials, such as metal, wood, and crops, for Roman manufactured goods such as pottery. Later they built their own workshops and ports and became trading centers in their own right. Eventually Rome bought more things from the provinces than it exported to them.

But the Romans did not just export their own culture. They also brought to Rome architecture, literature, and religion from the cultures they conquered. The republic copied boats from the Carthaginians, and Roman enthusiasm for the Greek language was such that the emperor Hadrian was said to have been more fluent in Greek than in Latin. Most of the slaves who taught young Roman boys were Greek. Even some of the religions of the conquered peoples were taken back to Rome and became very popular.

▶ *Roman architects and engineers traveled to all quarters of the empire. These are the remains of the forum in the Roman city at Sufetula in North Africa.*

The Social Ladder

Everyone had a place on the social ladder in Roman society. Of the million people who lived in Rome during the first century CE, most men were citizens and, as such, had rights and duties laid down by law. But not all citizens were equal. Every five years a census was taken in Rome, and men were assessed as to their status. There were three main classes of citizens. At the very top were the *nobiles*, who were the richest men and who were born into noble families. At first, only these men could become senators, but later any wealthy man who had proved himself to be a good citizen could be a senator. Below them were the *equites*, who were less wealthy and who were often businessmen. They could become magistrates. The third order of citizenship was the *plebs*, or *plebeians*.

There was a way for slaves to win their freedom; under the empire it became quite fashionable for wealthy men to free their slaves after a certain time or when a slave had saved enough money to buy his freedom. Then the slave became a freedman, and any children he had after that time became full Roman citizens. So, in theory, it would even be possible for these children to become senators when they grew up.

The *plebeians* were the commoners of the city, such as storekeepers, craftsmen, and agricultural workers.

There were millions of other people in the Roman Empire who were not included in these levels of citizenship. For example, women and children belonged to their husbands or fathers and had no rights of their own. People who lived in the Roman provinces had varying degrees of citizenship. In some provinces they were equal citizens, but they could not become *nobiles* or *equites*. In other provinces they could: Trajan and Hadrian, both from Spain, rose to the position of emperor. In some provinces, people had citizenship rights as regards trade and intermarriage, but they could not vote; and in others still, their citizenship was limited to paying taxes and providing men for the army.

In the worst position of all were the slaves. They were seen merely as possessions, owned entirely by their masters, who could do whatever they wanted to them. Varro, a writer from the first century CE, called slaves "a species of articulate farming stock," which was his way of saying that they were like farm animals that could speak. Most of the hard labor in Rome was carried out by slaves.

▼ *Two household slaves go about their daily routine. Slaves worked on farms, in mines and factories, and on building sites. They maintained the water supply, worked as clerks, teachers, actors, doctors, and artists.*

Religion in Rome

Gods and Goddesses

Ancient Rome had many magnificent temples dedicated to the huge family of gods in the state religion. Jupiter, who represented justice and honor, was the most powerful. His brothers were Dis, the god of the underworld, and Neptune, the god of the sea. His sisters, Vesta and Ceres, were responsible for the hearth and agriculture, and his wife, Juno, protected women and childbirth. Jupiter's children were Vulcan, the god of craftsmen, and Mars, who was the god of war and the father of Romulus and Remus. Diana was the goddess of hunters, and her sister, Minerva, was the goddess of crafts and wisdom. Mercury was the god of trade, and Bacchus was the god of wine. The god of prophecy and healing was Apollo.

Each god could be asked for help by performing a sacrifice at the god's temple. The temples were guarded by priests and priestesses who also conducted the ceremonies. The Romans believed that sacrifices were very important to the gods. If something went wrong during the ceremony, it had to be done all over again.

▶ *Sacrifices to Mars were usually a pig, a sheep, and an ox, but on October 15 every year, the winning male racehorse at the Circus Maximus was slaughtered in Mars's honor.*

The Romans believed that priests could tell what was going to happen in the future by examining the insides of the animals that they sacrificed. There were also prophets who looked into the future by examining the sky, birds in flight, cloud formations, and lightning. In times of national emergency a very special set of books, written by a prophetess named the Sybil, could be consulted. Before any battle, the generals always consulted some special hens that had been blessed by a priest. The hens were given corn, and if they refused to eat, the battle would be lost. The writer Suetonius tells the story of one general who ignored the warning: "He began a sea battle though the sacred chickens had refused to eat. In contempt of religious practices, he threw the chickens into the sea, remarking that if they did not eat they could drink." He recalls that the general lost 93 ships and their crews in that battle and barely escaped with his own life.

Bulls, sheep, and pigs were often sacrificed, and their organs were inspected for signs that would show whether or not the gods were pleased.

The Romans believed that there were spirits all around them. A rock or a stream or even a door had its own spirit. In the home, Janus, who had two heads (and gave his name to the first month of the year), was the god who guarded the door, while other gods called the penates guarded the larder. Also in the house were the spirits of dead ancestors. Tiny statues of them were kept in a closet and worshiped.

Foreign Religions

The Romans tolerated other religions in their city. As foreigners came and settled in Rome, they brought their religions with them, and the government was generally happy to allow this.

One imported goddess was Cybele, the Great Mother. She was a popular goddess with women, because she was believed to help them in childbirth and with their general health. The religion originally came from Asia Minor (modern Turkey) in about 204 BCE. The ceremonies included dancing and sacrifices, and, to make up for sins they had committed, women were often sent to bathe in the freezing Tiber, or they had to go to a distant temple to bring back holy water.

Isis was another imported goddess, this time from Egypt. She was ruler of all heaven and earth. Another new religion was popularized when the Egyptian Queen Cleopatra visited Rome in 45 BCE. This cult celebrated the death and rebirth of the consort of Isis, a young man named Osiris.

The Romans first came across Judaism when they invaded Palestine in 63 BCE, and at first the religion was tolerated. The Emperor Augustus even decreed that Jews did not have to appear in court on their Sabbath. Jews came to Rome to live, and many Romans were converted to Judaism. But their religion said that they could only worship one god, and the Romans wanted to put statues of their divine emperors into the synagogues. The Jews refused, and Judaism was eventually banned in Rome.

▲ *A head of the Persian god Mithras. Mithras was originally a sun god. In the initiation ceremony, his worshipers were baptized in the blood of a bull. Sinners were punished in the afterlife by hellfire.*

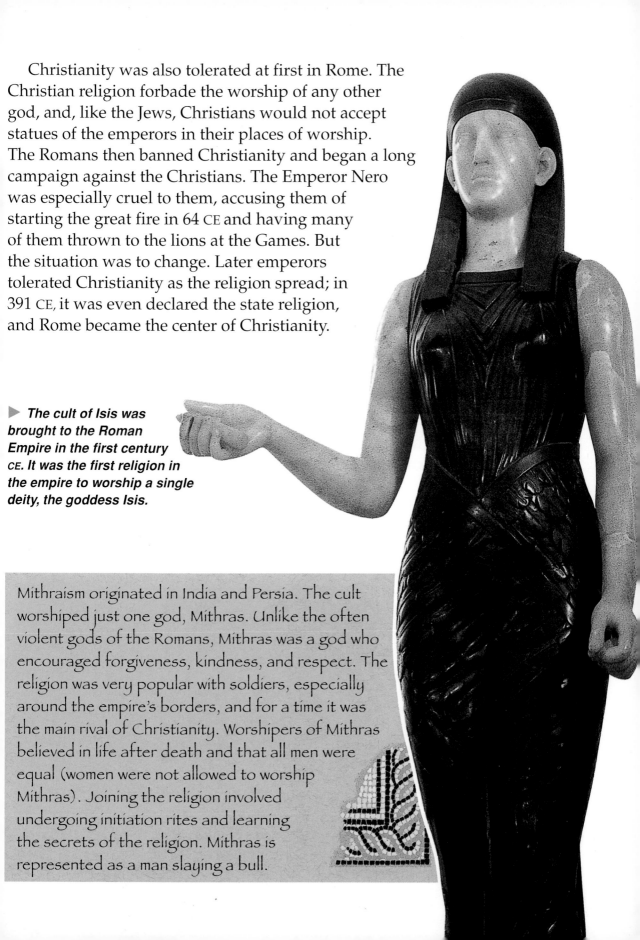

Christianity was also tolerated at first in Rome. The Christian religion forbade the worship of any other god, and, like the Jews, Christians would not accept statues of the emperors in their places of worship. The Romans then banned Christianity and began a long campaign against the Christians. The Emperor Nero was especially cruel to them, accusing them of starting the great fire in 64 CE and having many of them thrown to the lions at the Games. But the situation was to change. Later emperors tolerated Christianity as the religion spread; in 391 CE, it was even declared the state religion, and Rome became the center of Christianity.

▶ *The cult of Isis was brought to the Roman Empire in the first century CE. It was the first religion in the empire to worship a single deity, the goddess Isis.*

Mithraism originated in India and Persia. The cult worshiped just one god, Mithras. Unlike the often violent gods of the Romans, Mithras was a god who encouraged forgiveness, kindness, and respect. The religion was very popular with soldiers, especially around the empire's borders, and for a time it was the main rival of Christianity. Worshipers of Mithras believed in life after death and that all men were equal (women were not allowed to worship Mithras). Joining the religion involved undergoing initiation rites and learning the secrets of the religion. Mithras is represented as a man slaying a bull.

Art, Literature, and Technology

Architecture and Decoration

If you could go back in time to a Roman city, you would probably be amazed by the size and beauty of public buildings such as temples, public baths, and theaters. The Romans were able to build such huge and ornate buildings for three reasons. First, they learned how to build arches and vaults from the Etruscans. This allowed them to construct large round roofs, long bridges, and aqueducts. Second, from the Greeks they copied the rows of pillars that supported and decorated the roofs of the buildings. Finally, they had their own invention—concrete. This allowed them to build much bigger structures than would be possible with just stone blocks and mortar.

▼ *In the inaugural festival for the Colosseum, or Amphitheater Flavium, 100 days of continuous gladiatorial games and beast hunts took place. The stone to build it came from Tivoli, transported along a road specially built for that purpose. The three stories of columns are in different designs and the fourth story is a solid wall fitted with masts. These were used to pull out a huge canvas awning to keep the sun off spectators.*

► *Roman mosaics tell us a lot about Roman life. This one shows a Roman garrison detachment on the Nile. Here we can see troops among the lush greenery of Egypt.*

The Romans loved to decorate their buildings, using many different styles. The squares and temples were decorated with bronze and marble statues. To mark a particular victory in battle, the emperors often had columns erected, showing the battle and the spoils of war. One of these, which still stands, is Trajan's Column, which was erected to commemorate his conquest of Dacia. Walls might be decorated with bas relief carvings, which were statues partly carved out of marble blocks. Another form of wall decoration was the fresco, in which paint was applied to drying plaster walls. The most famous form of Roman decoration is the mosaic. To make a mosaic, thousands of tiny, colored tiles are set in a pattern into a cement base. They are often seen as floor coverings or wall decorations.

The Pantheon in Rome is a typical example of Roman architecture at its grandest. It was built in 25 BCE (as a temple), and later rebuilt around 124 CE by the Emperor Hadrian. It is a round, domed building 140 ft. (43 m) in diameter and 140 ft. (43 m) high. At the very top is a hole in the roof, 28 ft. (8.5 m) in diameter, to let in light. Its walls were lined with marble, and inside it were statues of the gods. Huge bronze doors are still in place today.

Another vast building in Rome was the Basilica Julia, which was a single hall with colonnades occupying an area of 328 ft. (100 m) by 120 ft. (36 m). Roman theaters were equally huge. They were built as semicircles, and their great height was made possible by a series of arches that supported the weight of the building. The most famous Roman building of all, the Colosseum, was commissioned by the Emperor Titus. It is an oval 656 ft. (200 m) long. It held 45,000 spectators and was built entirely of stone, in three tiers of arches.

Technology

As we have seen, the Romans used arches and concrete in their buildings. Besides these, they had many other inventive building techniques. One of the things that they always needed to do was to bring a fresh water supply into the city. As early as the fourth century BCE, they did this by building aqueducts, which carried water for miles. These were always on a slight slope, so that water would run downhill all the way into the city.

Aqueducts were built on arches, which needed a minimum of building materials, so that the weight of the structure would not make it unstable. By the first century CE, there were eight aqueducts providing water for the Romans, extending over 50 mi. (80 km). They were built over hundreds of years, to keep pace with the increasing population of Rome. When the Romans had to bring water uphill, they made waterwheels. Here a system of wheels, turned by slaves, brought the water up from one level to the next.

▼ *The Pont du Gard, at Nimes in France, has three tiers of arches that carried a water channel 165 ft. (50 m) above the river. It was probably built some time in the second century CE, under the rule of the Emperor Antoninus.*

Bridge-building techniques were also very ingenious. First they put a wooden bridge over the river, supported by a series of anchored boats. Then they drove wooden stakes into the riverbed, making the frame for a pillar. The water was pumped out of this wooden frame, and blocks of stone were put inside. Wooden frames were then built between the stone pillars, and stone arches were built over them.

Many building techniques used by the Romans were the forerunners of much of the technology that we use today. The Romans used simple wooden cranes, driven by slaves in a treadmill, to lift heavy objects. Scaffolding was also erected on the sides of buildings, for workmen to walk on. Walls were built of brick or stone. The inside walls were often wooden frames filled with rubble and covered with a surface layer of plaster. The builders' tools were also remarkably similar to those we use today. From a Roman workman's toolbag we would recognize planes, pliers, trowels, axes, and many other things.

▲ *This illustration, from a builder's tomb, shows a Roman crane. At the bottom slaves are inside the treadmill, winding ropes in a pulley system. The crane was used to lift large stones into place.*

After the water had traveled from its source in the hills to the city, it was piped into large storage tanks. From there, more pipes carried it to the city's fountains, public toilets, and baths. The pipes were made of sections of lead bent into tubes and fitted together. Most people collected their water from the public fountains, although the very rich often bribed the slaves who worked on the water system to pipe a supply into their private houses. Waste water was carried away by a series of sewer pipes. In apartment buildings, called insulae, there would be a pipe into which tenants could throw their waste. This flowed out into the gutter and down into the sewers. Excavated streets in Ostia or Pompeii still have stepping-stones across the roads; they were there so that people did not have to walk through the waste water.

Roman Writers

Ancient Rome produced many writers who were very influential men in their times, and whose surviving works are still very well thought of today. Some of them wrote plays that were performed in theaters all over the Roman Empire. The performances, which were free to all citizens, were paid for by rich men; they often did so hoping that the public would be grateful and would vote for them at election time. We still have 20 comedies written by Plautus. He was a poor man who worked in a bakery until he had his first play performed. His plays are very funny, with lots of slapstick comedy, and characters that the people of Rome would recognize from their daily lives, such as scheming slaves or nosy neighbors. Shakespeare used one of Plautus's stories as a model when he wrote his play *The Comedy of Errors*. Terence was another very famous comic playwright. He began life as a slave and wrote only six plays before being killed in a shipwreck at the age of 26.

Catullus and Horace are two famous Roman poets who expressed their feelings about life and their fellow citizens in their poetry. Catullus came from quite a wealthy family. He wrote very romantic poetry to his mistress, whom he called Lesbia, in his poems. Horace was the son of a freed slave.

▶ *The actors in Plautus's and Terence's plays wore masks. Each kind of mask represented a different type of character and would be easily recognized by the audience. Other stage props included a complex system of backdrops, which could be raised and lowered behind the actors. The first stone theater was built by Pompey in 55 CE. It held 27,000 people, many fewer than most amphitheaters held.*

Pliny lived during the rule of Nero and Vespasian. He came from a wealthy family and was himself an important member of the government. He is remembered for his *Natural History*, which is a book about the natural sciences: biology, geology, and geography. He spent all his time reading or making notes on what he read. He loved to research everything himself. In 79 CE, he went to see the eruption of the volcano Vesuvius, and while trying to get close to the eruptions, he was choked to death by the fumes.

Horace had worked as a clerk until a rich nobleman, who liked his poetry, decided to give him enough money to give up his job to write poetry. Horace wrote about everyday things: too much garlic in food, boring people, and advice to the young. Ovid was also a brilliant poet; his poetry was often about Roman mythology and was very entertaining. Virgil wrote poetry about country life and the beauty of Italy. He also wrote about the glory of Rome in the *Aeneid*, the epic poem about the founding of Rome. He never finished this work but, nonetheless, it was published on the orders of the Emperor Augustus.

One reason we know so much about Rome is the work of the Roman historians. Julius Caesar wrote a history of his conquest of Gaul, while Livy wrote a history of Rome, starting from the arrival of Aeneas to his own day. Tacitus, a senator and governor of Asia, was also a famous historian, but unfortunately only a few of his books have survived. Most of what is known of the history of Roman Britain is from Tacitus's biography of his father-in-law, Agricola, who was governor of Britain for a time.

Everyday Life

The Roman Family

At the head of the Roman family was the *paterfamilias*; he was the husband and father, and the master of his slaves. Roman families were generally small, with perhaps two or three children. Newborn girls or boys with birth defects were often left to die. People wanted sons rather than daughters because only sons could inherit the family's wealth. If a family had no son, the father would adopt one. Divorce was common, and when it happened the children always stayed with their father.

In rich families, the wife supervised her children's upbringing, but women from poorer families often had jobs. Women could work in stores, taverns, markets, or even at the baths. A few women became doctors or lawyers, and in later times some even acted in the theater. Roman women were often thought to be more learned than men—they were well educated and had more spare time to study and read.

Roman children had many different kinds of toys. Girls played with rag dolls or carved stone or pottery figures and buildings; some wooden dolls with hinged arms and legs have been found. Boys played with marbles, kites, hoops, and tops. They also played war games with wooden swords and shields. In one popular game, called Jacks, each player threw stones into the air and tried to catch them on the back of the hand. Board games were very popular in Rome. A game similar to checkers has been discovered in many places. Games of chance, such as *capita et navia* (heads or tails, played with coins), and dice games were also common with both children and adults. At the Roman remains at Bath in the west of England, a pair of loaded dice have been found.

▲ *These children are taking part in a religious procession. The early years were difficult for Roman children. If they were not abandoned at birth, they still stood a good chance of dying from one of many childhood diseases.*

Both boys and girls received educations in Rome. At elementary level, boys and girls went separately to a *litterator*, who taught them reading, writing, and arithmetic. Once they reached 12 or 13, the girls stayed home and had private tuition. Boys were then taught history, geography, astronomy, and literature by a teacher called a *grammaticus*. Once he was 16, a boy became a citizen. From the age of 16, he could go to a *rhetor*, where he was taught public speaking. Most children in Roman times were engaged at 14 or 15. The marriage ceremony was at the bride's home. After the sacrifice of an animal, friends and relatives witnessed the couple's exchange of vows. Following a feast at the bride's home, a procession would go to the groom's house, where the bride was carried over the threshold.

When a wealthy man died, his body would lie in state for a few days so people could come and pay their respects. After that the body was carried outside the city for burial or cremation, accompanied by mourners, musicians, and torch bearers. A tomb would be erected to the man's memory. When people were cremated, food and clothes were thrown onto a fire for their use in the afterlife. The poor were buried in common pits.

Daily Life

The Roman working day began at dawn with the sounds of builders and repairmen in the street and slaves in the house. Getting out of bed and dressed was simple since both men and women slept naked and simply put on their garments and slippers. A wash in a basin kept them going until the afternoon when they would visit the public baths. Rich women were made up and had their hair styled by their slaves. After a simple breakfast of bread and fruit, the day's work began. Working people went off to their workplace for the day. The unemployed went as early as possible to the house of a patron (someone who was prepared to give them money and support in exchange for their loyalty).

Every morning, between 7 and 9 A.M., these rich men, or patrons, interviewed their clients and gave them money or advice. Children from poor families often worked alongside their parents to bring in extra money. Wealthier boys went to schools that began at dawn and lasted until noon.

Lunch for everyone was another light meal of bread, cheese, fish, and vegetables. Since the working people in Rome had no kitchens, they ate at food stands. Very poor people lived on handouts of grain and bread.

The hot Roman afternoons were dedicated to a rest, or siesta, or perhaps a visit to the baths.

▼ *These Roman baths are at Bath in England. Called Aquae Sulis, the baths were dedicated to the goddess Minerva and were built over natural hot springs.*

In the evenings people would have their main meal. For the rich families this consisted of three courses, eaten in a formal dining room called a *triclinium*. In the room were three couches arranged around a low table. People lay down on these couches to eat their food. The poor again bought food from food stands. Most people went to bed by dusk because the streets of Rome were dangerous after dark; there was no street lighting and heavy traffic jammed the streets.

Every Roman city had several bathhouses. They were inexpensive to visit, sometimes even free, and were used by everyone; men on one day and women on another. The baths consisted of a series of rooms of varying temperatures, heated by a *hypocaust* system (see page 45). A bather gradually went from the *frigidarium* (the coolest room) to the *tepidarium* and then the *caldarium* (the hottest room). Slaves were on hand to oil the skin and scrape away the day's dirt. After washing in a hot bath, the bather would return to the *frigidarium* for a cold plunge. People went to the baths to meet friends, have business meetings, and catch up on the latest gossip. There were also rooms where you could sit quietly, exercise areas, and gardens to walk in. Only the very rich had their own baths because everyone enjoyed visiting the public baths.

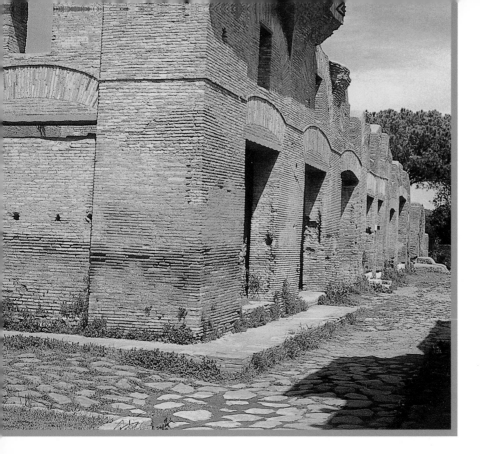

City Life

At its peak, Rome was so crowded that most people lived in *insulae*, apartment buildings of five or six stories. Between the buildings were narrow alleyways that let in hardly any sunlight. The upper floors had no running water or sanitation, so people collected their water from public fountains, used public toilets, and threw their waste out of their windows or into a well inside the building. To us, Rome would have seemed a noisy, smelly place. During the day it was so busy that vehicles were banned, and goods could be brought into the city only at night.

The heart of the city was the Forum, an impressive open space where public meetings were held. Around the Forum were the Basilicas where law courts were held. Scattered throughout the city were the huge public buildings erected by the various emperors and the temples to the gods. Beside these were the *insulae*. Their lower stories were stores or businesses or even the imposing apartments of rich people.

The Villa Julia Felix and its garden were built in Pompeii. Pompeii was a small provincial city whose chief product was cloth. Houses there were built in a quadrangle style enclosing a small garden.

44

Poorer people lived above the first floor and had no cooking facilities. The *insulae* often collapsed or burned down. Alongside them, the houses of the rich were low buildings with windowless outer walls. Inside was an open courtyard with a pool, the *impluvium*, to catch rainwater. Around the courtyard were the dining room, kitchen, toilet, and various sitting rooms. The house was entered by a gate in the wall. The family shrine was in the garden behind the house. In some of the colder countries of the empire, the house was heated by a hypocaust system. Air, warmed by a furnace, traveled around underfloor passages and up through ducts in the walls.

Fires were a daily occurrence in Rome. The poet Juvenal wrote: "No, no, I must live where there is no fire and the night is free from alarms." The upper stories of buildings were mostly made of wood and had no water supply. They were heated, if at all, by open braziers of coal and lit by oil lamps. Fire fighting consisted of teams of slaves or soldiers forming chains with buckets of water.

Country Life

Many wealthy Roman citizens had houses in the countryside. After the wars with Carthage it became fashionable when generals retired—with lots of booty from the wars—to build great country estates. Their villas were enclosed by walls; at one end of the enclosure was the villa where the owner lived; at the other end would be the buildings where the slaves and animals lived. There was a storehouse, rooms for fermenting wine and pressing olive oil, and a bathhouse, which would be used by both the owner and the servants. Around the villa, olives, grapes, figs, vegetables, and grain were grown. Bees were kept for their honey, and there would usually be large herds of pigs, because pork was the favorite meat of the Romans. Sheep and goats were kept to produce wool, rope, and milk, while cattle and donkeys were beasts of burden.

▶ *This mosaic, from Tunis in North Africa, shows the activities of a working villa. The villa in the center is surrounded by scenes of agricultural life: slaves gathering food, undertaking administration tasks, hunting, and looking after livestock.*

▼ *People who lived in the city, like the Emperor Hadrian, often had villas in the countryside. Hadrian's villa was so imposing that it was more of a palace than a country home.*

Pigeons, ducks, geese, and hens were kept on the estates for food and feathers.

Whether on a large estate or a tiny farm, many of the tools that Roman farmers used were very similar to the ones still used today. To till the soil they used a plow pulled by oxen. To break up stony land they had picks. The crops were harvested by using a sickle, and some of the big farms had threshing machines. Flour mill wheels were turned by animals such as donkeys. Wine was a favorite product of Italy, and grapes were grown on many farms; when they were ripe, grapes were put into a stone trough and stepped on to extract the juice. The Romans were sophisticated farmers; they practiced crop rotation to improve the soil.

Hadrian's Villa at Tivoli, northeast of Rome, is a fine example of a Roman villa at its most impressive. Besides the usual rooms, the villa had a library, a theater, and a stadium, and the gardens around his house covered an area of 11 sq mi. (18 sq km).

In a book on farm management written by Marcus Cato, the duties of a farm manager, who was usually a slave, are described:

"The farm manager must not be an idler. ... He must be the first to rise in the morning and the last to bed. He must see that the farm is shut up and that everyone is asleep in the right place and the animals have fodder."

In his book on farm management, Cato advises on the best treatment of slaves. He says exactly how much bread each slave should have daily during the winter and suggests an increase when slaves begin to work in the vineyards. He also recommends that slaves should get a new set of clothes every two years. The slaves who worked on these farms had hard lives, often kept in chain gangs and locked up at night to prevent them from escaping.

▲ This is part of a floor mosaic, perhaps from a dining room. It shows seafood delicacies such as lobster, octopus, and eels. These might have been part of the main course of the meal, served in rich sauces. Some people enjoyed their food so much that they took medicine halfway through to make themselves vomit. Then they could go back and start all over again!

Food

The type of food eaten by the citizens of Rome was determined by how rich they were. Very poor people were given free handouts of grain or bread and sometimes even wine and oil. City working people bought cooked food from stands in the street: circular loaves of bread, hot cooked turnips, eggs, sausages, or pureed peas. Meat was rarely eaten. Rich people had teams of slaves to prepare elaborate, sumptuous meals. Their food was cooked in spices and herbs such as coriander, nutmeg, cumin, ginger, mint, and thyme and served with fish or fruit sauces. Some slaves spent their whole day preparing the evening meal for their masters.

The evening meal consisted of three courses. Appetizers were items like salad or snails or shellfish. Wine sweetened with honey was served after this. The next course was several dishes of different meats served with vegetables and sauces. The last course might be fruit, honey and cakes, or stuffed dates. Wine was served throughout the meal. During a dinner party there would usually be a poetry reading or musical performance of some kind.

Clothes

Roman men wore quite simple clothes. Their underwear was just loincloths, and over those they wore short, woolen tunics. When they went out they wore togas—large sheets of cloth draped in elaborate folds around the shoulders. Most people hated to wear them, and various emperors had to pass laws forcing men to put on their togas for public occasions. In Britain and other cold areas of the empire, men needed to wear tight-fitting leggings, warm socks, and even waterproof capes.

In the early days of the empire Roman women wore their hair in simple knots, but later elaborate braids and curls and blonde or red wigs were popular. Women used ash or antimony (a type of metal) to darken their eyelids and the sediment from red wine or red ocher for lipstick. They often covered their faces with powdered chalk to whiten them and carried little sets of tools for plucking hair and cleaning out ears. Jewelry was important. Women often wore earrings made of gold set with precious stones and gold link chains around their necks. Brooches might be precious gems or cameos carved from sardonyx. Women also wore anklets and bracelets; a snake design was very popular for these. It was the custom to wear a wedding ring and probably several other rings, often between the first and second joints of the fingers.

▲ *Heated metal curling tongs were used to create complicated hairstyles like this one. Red or blonde hair for making wigs was often taken from the heads of foreign slaves.*

Women wore loincloths and something like brassieres. Over these they, too, wore tunics. Married women wore another gown called a *stola*, which was a long overdress. When they went out women wore *pallas*, which were shawls that they draped in various styles around their shoulders and heads.

Entertainment

The most popular forms of entertainment in ancient Rome were chariot racing and the Games. They took place on the 150 or more annual public holidays that Rome had. They were paid for by rich men or by the government, who wanted to keep the poor people of Rome contented. These big spectacles were immensely popular. In 160 BCE, during a performance of a play by Terence, someone announced that the chariot races were starting, and the entire audience ran out of the theater. The chariot races took place at the Circus Maximus, with slaves as drivers. If they were successful these slaves grew very rich and famous; but the chariots often crashed, and the drivers were killed or injured. Fans of one chariot team would often get into fights with fans of another.

▼ *In the chariot races, teams of four horses pulled a tiny chariot driven by a slave. This course has three pillars at each end and in the middle a man is counting the laps. Three of the seven laps have been run in this picture since there are four markers still left. At the three pillars, the chariots had to make a 180° turn, which was very dangerous—many men were killed doing it.*

The Games were held in the Colosseum and were even more horrific. Criminals or slaves were given weapons and put into the ring to fight to the death. They were called gladiators. Those who refused to fight were pushed into the ring with red-hot irons.

▶ *Armed gladiators fighting wild animals. Often the humans would be bound to stakes and left to be torn apart, but here they are able to defend themselves.*

Although many gladiators became rich and famous and received their freedom, life was desperate for most of them. In 73 BCE, a group of gladiators in Capua broke out of their prison and escaped. They were led by a man from Thrace, named Spartacus. He had fought for the Roman army and had considerable skills as a general. He knew that if he was caught he would be killed. Thousands of slaves all over Italy deserted from their farms and joined him. Roman armies were sent out to capture them and were beaten. The band of runaways rampaged around the countryside, traveling north toward the Alps and robbing farms on their way. Spartacus tried to persuade them to flee over the Alps to freedom, but many of them were enjoying their lives as bandits too much. They were eventually defeated, and while most, including Spartacus, fought to the death, 6,000 were captured and crucified along the main road into Rome, as a warning to other slaves.

At the Games an unarmed man was usually pitted against one in armor. Often men were put into the arena so the audience could watch them being mauled to death by wild animals. In 80 CE, 5,000 wild animals and 4,000 tame animals were killed in just one day.

In a very popular form of the Games, the Colosseum was flooded, or a nearby lake was used, and teams of slaves in boats fought one another. People enjoyed betting on the races and games. Spectators occasionally got injured. Once, in 27 CE, an entire amphitheater collapsed, killing 50,000 people. Another time a herd of elephants stampeded, breaking down the barriers that protected the crowds and injuring many people.

Decline and Fall

Decline of the Empire

As the empire grew and grew, many things changed in Rome—not always for the better. Ambitious soldiers and provincial governors fought to be the next emperors. As we have seen, many of the emperors were bad, while some were good administrators who strengthened the empire. After the death of Marcus Aurelius, Rome was plagued by a series of poor rulers. The first of these was Marcus Aurelius's son, Commodus, who ruled Rome for 12 years and was one of the worst emperors that the empire had ever seen. He was eventually assassinated by the Praetorian Guard, who auctioned off the job of emperor to the highest bidder! During the following century so much time was spent fighting over who would be emperor that little attention was paid to the far reaches of the empire.

In Germany, local tribes called the Goths, the Franks, and the Alamanni banded together and began to threaten Roman territory.

Marcus Aurelius, a Spaniard from Cordoba, served as emperor from 161 CE to 180 CE. He was a very shy man who, before becoming emperor, had spent his life studying philosophy. He inherited an empire that had little money to spend and several wars to fight. One of his ways of finding cash was to sell off the imperial jewels. He oversaw a war against the Parthians in 163–164 CE, and although his troops were successful, they brought a terrible plague back to Rome, which spread across the empire and killed thousands of people. On the German front, Marcus Aurelius sent troops against the Marcomanni and Quadi tribes and defeated them. He built a column in Rome to celebrate his victory. During his time as emperor he wrote a book of philosophy, in Greek.

In Parthia there were constant battles, and in 259 CE, the Emperor Valerian was actually captured by the Persians. In 270 CE, the Emperor Aurelian abandoned Dacia and concentrated his efforts on defeating the Alamanni on the German border. He also reconquered Gaul, which had declared itself independent of Rome. Then Queen Zenobia of Palmyra, to the east of the empire, began attacks on Egypt and Asia Minor. She was defeated by Aurelian, and her city was destroyed. Aurelian remained emperor for 14 years, but he, too, was assassinated.

▼ *Zenobia was Queen of Palmyra, the oasis city in northern Arabia, which was a vital stopping point on the Roman caravan routes. The city was destroyed after its attacks on the empire.*

◄ *Marcus Aurelius's column in Rome was erected in 176 CE. It celebrates his triumph over the Marcomanni. Near the top we can see soldiers holding their shields in a tortoise formation. The shields are locked together in a defensive posture.*

A Divided Empire

After the assassination of Aurelian in 275 CE, there was another scramble for power, and Rome became very unstable once again. Food prices began to rise, and heavy taxes were introduced. Bands of outlaws began to roam around the empire, and fresh invasions took place near the borders. In 284 CE Diocletian came to power. His solution to the problem of keeping the empire together was to split it into two sections—the east and the west—and to have two emperors. He strengthened the army, set maximum prices for food,

and set a limit for wage rises. His solutions did little to solve any of Rome's problems, but they did make the army more powerful and dangerous. The senate lost a lot of its power during this period. Black markets for food and other goods began. Diocletian declared himself a god and in 305 CE retired to a great palace in the modern town of Split in Croatia. Chaos broke out again, with up to four contenders for the job of emperor at any one time, until in 312 CE the general in charge of Britain, Constantine, returned to Rome to claim the throne. After winning a battle with his chief rival for power in Rome, Maxentius, he declared tolerance for all religious groups. He slowly reunited the various parts of the empire, brought in higher taxes, made the army more powerful, and took away many of the freedoms that Romans were used to. But his measures did not restore the strength of the empire.

Christians had been persecuted in the Roman Empire since the very early days. Despite this, Christianity had grown. When Constantine left Britain and was about to begin the battle for Rome, he thought he saw a vision in the sky. He believed he saw a cross, and the words *in hoc signo vinces*, meaning "you will conquer with this sign." After his success in battle Constantine allowed Christians to worship one god. Later he even made himself the head of the Christian church in Rome. Now the state god—the emperor—was also the leader of the Christians, and this made Christianity much more important in the Roman Empire. Constantine adopted the Christian symbol of the first two letters of Christ's name. They are **X** (chi) and **P** (rho) in the Greek alphabet. They can be seen in many decorations of the time.

▼ *The remains of a once huge statue of Constantine that was probably worshiped as the image of a god.*

The western part of the empire was constantly under attack from the Barbarians (the word the Romans used for the various tribes around their borders). Constantine realized that he could not prevent Rome from being taken, so he moved his capital city away from Rome to Byzantium in the east and renamed it Constantinople. In that way he kept the Roman Empire alive for another thousand years.

The Sack of Rome

Constantine chose his three sons to become emperors after him, but the empire quickly fell victim to more power struggles. The worst threat to the empire, especially the western half of it, was invasion. A tribe of nomads from the east, called the Huns, were moving across Europe looking for fresh land; as they marched on, they chased the German tribes in front of them.

The Emperor Justinian was the son of a Slav peasant. Also shown in the mosaic is his general Belisarius. The name Maximian appears above the archbishop.

Tribes such as the Vandals, Visigoths, and Suebi fled to the empire for protection from the Huns and were allowed to settle there. They joined the Roman armies. Later, even Huns who had crossed into Roman territory were allowed to stay and defend the borders. Weak emperors had no finances to drive out the enemies of Rome, so they were forced to accept them.

In 402 CE, Italy was invaded by the Goths. Rome was still the capital of the western empire, but the emperor, Honorius, was afraid and moved to Ravenna on the east coast of Italy. In 409 CE Vandals invaded Spain. The following year Rome was sacked and looted by the Goths, and the Roman legions were withdrawn from Britain to defend Italy.

Constantine's foresight in moving the capital of the empire to safety, in Byzantium, meant that while Roman buildings and laws fell apart in the west, the east was flourishing. Latin died out as the dominant language and was replaced by Greek, and art and architecture gradually grew away from their Roman origins. The last great emperor of Constantinople was Justinian, from 527 CD to 565 CE. He sent troops back to Europe to reclaim the western empire. But the cost of the operation was much too high, and too much damage had been done in Rome and the great cities of North Africa. Within 100 years the cities were all lost again. Justinian also reformed and rewrote all the Roman laws, and his legal code is the basis of modern European law today.

Northern Europe was then taken over by the Franks, North Africa by the Vandals, and France by Attila the Hun. Finally Ravenna, the new capital, was taken and the emperor was deposed in 476 CE. This signaled the absolute end of the original western Roman Empire.

▼ *By 500 CE, the Roman Empire existed only in the east, and western Europe was divided into smaller kingdoms ruled by the invaders from the north.*

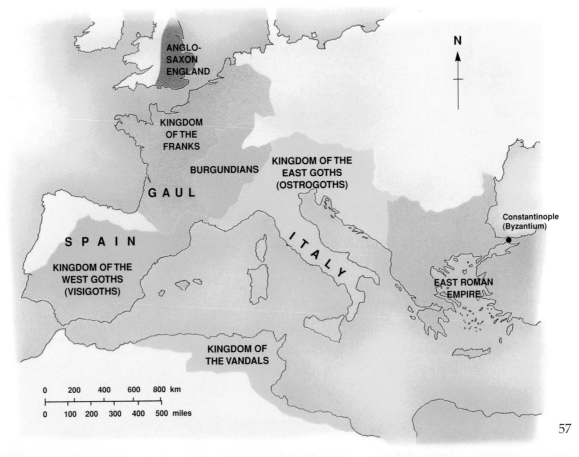

ANGLO-SAXON ENGLAND

KINGDOM OF THE FRANKS

BURGUNDIANS

KINGDOM OF THE EAST GOTHS (OSTROGOTHS)

GAUL

SPAIN

ITALY

KINGDOM OF THE WEST GOTHS (VISIGOTHS)

Constantinople (Byzantium)

EAST ROMAN EMPIRE

KINGDOM OF THE VANDALS

N

| 0 | 200 | 400 | 600 | 800 km |
| 0 | 100 | 200 | 300 | 400 | 500 miles |

The Roman Legacy

Roman Influence

Roman civilization lasted for over 1,000 years and affected the lives of millions of people. It brought cities to rural Europe and brought people who were hundreds of miles apart, with different languages and beliefs, into one big community. Strangely, when the Romans withdrew from a city their technology left with them, and people fell back into barbarism. Their beautiful buildings could not be maintained, their plumbing fell into disrepair, and their aqueducts stopped working.

Even today the Romans influence our daily lives. The language that we speak has many of its roots in Latin. The Roman name for an apartment building, *insula*, meaning a building separated from those around it, has given us the word "insulate." The Roman common man, *plebeian*, has come directly into our language and has also given us the word "plebiscite," meaning a vote taken by all the people. The Roman word for father, *pater*, has given us many words like "paternal," "patriotic," "patronize," and "patron." It would be very difficult to speak even one sentence without using a word that has its roots in Latin. Other modern languages such as Spanish, French, and Italian are even closer to Latin.

Although the Roman Empire ended a long time ago, we know a great deal about it. When the Romans adopted Christianity, they set up many monasteries where monks spent a lot of their time copying famous books. Alongside Christian books, much of ancient Roman literature was also preserved, and that is how we know the history of ancient Rome.

▲ Roads built by the Romans, like this one in Yorkshire, England, have survived to the present day.

The Romans have left us many other things besides their language. The European legal system is based on the Roman one. Our ideas about government and legal institutions have also come from the Romans. Their contribution to transportation was great, too; Roman roads are still the basis of many European highways. Some Roman buildings are actually still in use, such as Diocletian's palace in Split. The jury system, the postal service, the fire department, daily newspapers, central heating, flushing toilets, and apartment buildings can all be traced back to the Romans as well.

▲ Communal public flushing toilets, such as this one, became common in Rome— even in private houses, where they could seat up to 20 people at a time. A channel of running water flows underneath the toilets, and a smaller channel can be seen in front of the toilets for washing after use.

We have also learned much about the Romans by looking at the ruins of their cities and towns. In marble statues we can see records of important events, or we can read the inscriptions on Roman graves. From the pictures on unearthed mosaic floors we can learn things about everyday life. An incredible piece of the past has been preserved in the remains of Pompeii. One afternoon in 79 CE, without warning, this town was covered with ash by the eruption of Mount Vesuvius, and left intact. The ash preserved the town exactly as it had been, with people going about their business. The town remains today, with food still on the tables, graffiti still on the walls, and houses laid out as they were on the day of the eruption. Even people and dogs, running away from the horror of the volcano, were covered with ash and lie exactly where they died centuries ago. Today tourists walk among the ruins of the town and imagine the Romans going about their daily routines.

▼ *This is one of the 2,000 or more residents of Pompeii who didn't make it to the boats in time. He was probably suffocated by the ash that fell on the city, eventually covering it.*

Timeline

133 Plans to reallocate land in Rome to the poor are abandoned.
73 Slave revolt led by Spartacus.
67 Pompey is given the task of getting rid of pirates in the Mediterranean.
58 Gaius Julius Caesar is made governor of Gaul.

BCE
753 According to legend, Rome is founded by Romulus and Remus.
510 The Roman Republic established.
451 The Twelve Tablets are written down.
386 Rome is attacked by the Gauls.
367 The first plebeian is elected consul.
343–290 Wars against the Samnites.
282–275 Wars against the Greeks.
264–241 First war against Carthage.
238 Corsica and Sardinia become Roman provinces.
218–202 Hannibal's armies in Italy.
201 End of the second war against Carthage.
149–146 Last war against Carthage destroys city.

45 Julius Caesar takes power in Rome.
44 Julius Caesar is murdered.
31 Augustus becomes "first citizen."
4 The birth of Christ.

CE
29 Christ is crucified.
43 Claudius invades Britain.
64 Great Fire of Rome.
79 Eruption of Mount Vesuvius.
122 Hadrian's Wall is started.
376 Goths invade Italy and sack Rome.
395 The empire is divided.
476 The last Roman emperor is deposed.

Glossary

Amphitheater A round, roofless theater with steep banks of seats built around a circular arena. It was used for the Games.

Amphora A pottery jar used for storing liquids such as olive oil and wine.

Circus Maximus A huge chariot racing arena in Rome.

Consul The top government job in Rome, usually held by two men elected for one year.

Corbita A Roman trading ship.

Equites A class of Roman citizens made up of wealthy middle-class businessmen.

Etruscans People who settled in northwest and central Italy in 800 BCE. They were the early kings of Rome.

Fasces A bundle of rods with an ax in the middle, symbolizing the authority of a high magistrate.

Hastati Roman soldiers who wore light armor and carried swords and javelins.

Honestiores A class of person who would receive a light sentence for his crimes.

Humiliores A class of person who would be punished more heavily for his crimes.

Hypocaust Roman central heating using an underground furnace to send hot air under the floors of a building.

Insula A Roman apartment building.

Isis An Egyptian goddess worshiped by the Romans.

Lares Roman gods of the household.

Lictor A servant who carried the magistrate's fasces.

Mosaic A floor covering made of tiny pieces of tile or stone.

Nobiles The highest class of Roman citizen.

Papyrus Writing paper made from the leaves of a water plant from Egypt.

Paterfamilias The head of a Roman family.

Patricians The Roman upper class who in early times held power in Rome.

Penates Roman gods who protected a family's larder.

Plebeian A common working man.

Principes Roman soldiers armed with swords, spears, and shields.

Quadrangle A rectangular courtyard with buildings on all four sides.

Senate A council of 300 or more important citizens who advised the consuls or the emperor.

Strigil A curved scraper for cleaning the skin.

Theater A semicircular roofless building with steep banks of seats and a stage across the straight side. Plays were staged in the theater.

Toga A Roman man's outer garment.

Triarii Roman soldiers armed with spears and protected by armor.

Tribune Representative of the *Plebeians*, first elected in 490 BCE.

Triclinium A dining room with three sofas around a table.

Velites The poorest kind of Roman soldier with no armor, just a spear.

Further Reading and Web Sites

Books

Ancient Communities, Roman Life: Ancient Roman Homes
by Paul Harrison
PowerKids Press, 2010

The Romans: Life in Ancient Rome
by Liz Sonneborn
Millbrook Press, 2009

Understanding People in the Past: The Romans
by Rosemary Rees
Heinemann-Raintree, 2007

Web Sites

http://rome.mrdonn.org/index.html

http://www.historyforkids.org/learn/romans/index.htm

Index

Numbers in bold are illustrations